T0117088

Living Within My Thoughts

A Collection of Prose and Poetry

Sylva Caldwell

iUniverse, Inc.
New York Bloomington

Living Within My Thoughts
A Collection of Prose and Poetry

Copyright © 2009, Sylva Caldwell

All rights reserved. No part of this book may be used or reproduced by any means, graphic, electronic, or mechanical, including photocopying, recording, taping or by any information storage retrieval system without the written permission of the publisher except in the case of brief quotations embodied in critical articles and reviews.

iUniverse books may be ordered through booksellers or by contacting:

iUniverse
1663 Liberty Drive
Bloomington, IN 47403
www.iuniverse.com
1-800-Authors (1-800-288-4677)

Because of the dynamic nature of the Internet, any Web addresses or links contained in this book may have changed since publication and may no longer be valid. The views expressed in this work are solely those of the author and do not necessarily reflect the views of the publisher, and the publisher hereby disclaims any responsibility for them.

ISBN: 978-1-4401-1884-5 (sc)
ISBN: 978-1-4401-1885-2 (ebook)

Printed in the United States of America

iUniverse rev. date: 2/5/2009

Contents

Dedication

Tim I thank you for pushing and encouraging me to do what I had to do, in ways only a friend knows how.

Larry, you are the dearest and greatest friend. I thank you for your positive present in my life. I thank you for sharing your strength and knowledge.

Stepfon your insight is truly a value and I treasure our friendship. We have come a long way.

Alex, a.k.a. the Rooster. You have been with me through so much. I thank you for sharing your heart and your ear. I thank you for being my friend.

Epigraph

And it shall come to pass, that before they call, I will answer; and while they are yet speaking, I will hear.

(Isaiah 65:24)

Acknowledgments

I have to give thanks to our Lord and Savior for placing these words on my heart and mind that I am able to feel them intensely in my soul in order to share with others.

To my loving mother Annie, who shared her view on my drafts. Who encouraged and inspired me to use this gift. I love you with all my heart.

To Sandra, I am so bless we are sisters and best friends. Thank you so much for taking the time to read my words and giving me your honest opinion. Thank you for all your love, support and encouragement.

To Chante', and Akeem my daughter, and nephew. I love you both and thank you for being patient with me as I write my book. You both are great kids that I love dearly.

To Jackie, my dear sister I still miss you and I know your spirit is surrounding us. I love you big Sis.

To Grandmother, we truly miss you. You were and still are a great influence and role model in our lives. I miss your laughter and the way you use to call me Sylbo.

Every Man, Woman, and Child.

My Dedication

Only one deserves this high praise. As I think of whom to write this to, no one has been there more then you. You are the one who has pushed me through. My dedication is for you Lord for allowing these trials to be my testimonials. I pray I encourage others from my triumphs. Another gift was offer to me unwrapped and ready to be use.

No instruction was included, not sure on what to do. I prayed and slowly you showed me the way. All the tools I needed were in my reach. Once I grab my pen, grab my pad my writing was set on a new path. A new journey must begin.

Thank you my teacher, my leader, my Savior for all that you do. Thanks for placing the thoughts in my mind, to refresh it time after time. Thanks for the gentle words in my mouth that they can easily flow out. Thanks for blessing me with this spiritual pen and for not allowing the ink to never end.

My dedication is for you; please allow your spirit to be presence on each page from beginning to end. Let the readers know this gift is a blessing from you. Let their ears hear your voice. Let their heart feel your grace. Remind them that all things are possible when they place their faith with you and that they too have a purpose.

Stressing Over Some Mess

As I lay my head down to sleep, hoping to find some peace. Since my days were filled with worry over stressful mess. I toss I turn allowing this stress to bring me down, taking the best of me. Peace is all I seek.

Lord, what is wrong with me? Stressing over some mess and allowing my earthly possession to stretch my face with more lines. My beautiful hair is now growing gray, looking twice my age. So stressed out that my children's nerves are shaken listening to my high tone voice. Worrying over my lover because they are with another.

Lord you are the one that keeps me on my feet. Stressing over some mess, some of it I bought on myself. Always, whispering that silent cry. Help me Lord to get out of this mess. As I reach out my hand to pass it on. I feel your touch I hear your voice.

I Got This

I Got This

Stop your fear and stop your stressing. The Peace you seek is I. Welcome me to receive me; I will provide thee with the peace.

Watch me

I see you watching me. Near and far your eyes are covering me. Watching every movement and listening to my every word. Keep your eyes on me because I am coming through. Watch me as I come by to stop the show.

You watch me with anticipation waiting for the unveiling. You will never know what I will come up with next.. Open your eyes raise your blinds and watch me shine. Watch me as I move closer to our Father, who is watching over us all.

In the middle of it all

We allow ourselves to struggle with life problems. Confuse on what to do trying to handle it with manmade help. In the middle of it all, the Lord is waiting on your call. Listening and watching his child fall. Without him nothing can be done. He is the one we should call. We lay awake dreading the next day. Stressed and drain not even your dignity remain.

Weary and exhausted depression has set its mark. In the middle of it all, the Lord is waiting on your call. We feel he should come to us within the second. Blinded by doubt not recognizing what his power is about. In the middle of it all, the Lord has been waiting on your call. He knows what is right for you. He will answer your prayers when you stop putting him in the middle and place him on top.

Think about it

Should we live above our means or should we live by faith and truthfully believe the Lord will make a way? Do we live poorly because of the choices we have made or are we so afraid to step out of the box to enrich our lives?

Why must we blame others for our shortcomings because we are judge by the color of our skin?

How long will you give in to your circumstances and accept it as it is. Will you continue to stand in that line with your hand held out or will you finally rise up and unleash those ideas that you have been dreaming about.

Can you really push yourself to the limit to make a better life or will you just wait around because you feel there is no better way out. Laziness keeps you from learning more because the only books you have are about fancy house ware. Why are you so terrified to dare? Do you really think the Lord want us to be poor? Believe me you can have a better life, if you stop thinking about it and just do it.

Imagine

Waking up to the beauty of the Sun. Resting with the light of the Moon. Can you imagine the authority that controls the twinkling of the Stars? With the opening of his hand, he can make beaches with sand. A holy spirit that heals your aches and pain.

Close your eyes and imagine that power that lives with you and me. From the softness of his voice, he can make the waters be still. Can you imagine such power, a mighty power that requires faith to believe? A mystery for those who do not.

Can you imagine if you truly pray in the right way, He will surely make a way? All over the world, he exists. Choosing him is what he asks. Placing trust in him will turn your life around.

Can you feel the presence of Angels that listen to him? Father, Son, and Holy Ghost he is the light. Can you imagine a drop of rain, blowing of the wind is managed by him? Calling out his name will chase out wicked things. Just imagine life without him. Can you imagine?

A good man

Let me clarify let me break this down. Through my years, I have found there are still some good men around. They come in different shapes and styles. Let me explain as I sort them out. Open your mind and be aware there are some who would try to pull the wool over your eyes. They have wondering spirits, some good some bad. Some know the Lord, some wish they had. Know these men and know them well. Some feel no need to supply. They will watch the kids while you struggle to provide. They will pay the bills with the money you made. Love you deeply when you protest. Drive your car and stay out nightly. While he brags to the boys how he got you in place. You welcome him because you are just glad you have a man living at your address. They are the Sorry Man.

There are some with loud actions. They love you one minute and the next they will not. Yet you are still certain this is it. In private, you are his chick in public you will not be miss. You hold on because you believe them when they say they are just scared of being hurt so you stay. Hoping one-day love will find its way. One day you are the prize. Before you know it, you pushed aside. They are the Confuse Man.

Some will blame their own parents for their treatment so they mean no harm. They will bully you when they shout. You give them time instead of getting out. Their hands can be gentle. Say the wrong word they will get rough. You feel sorry thinking they will change. Spineless they are they will cowardly break you down and continue to hurt because they know you are not strong enough to walk away. They are the Abusive Man.

Some are fools who were too cool. They felt no need to finish school. You choose them thinking you will be safe because their pants were hanging beneath their waist. From every name in the book, they will call you out; with a smile, you still have no doubt. Calling you from lockup while fronting they are strong. Now they are crying home. In a few more days my man will be out how proudly you will say and sadly, you will wait. This a Trouble Man.

Some is neat to have a jack of all trade. They can make you laugh as they tune your car. He knows the name of every part with arms hard as steel and yet so tender with your heart. Do not take them for granted because they too are hard to find. They are a Handy Man.

Some have taken over your couch. Trash is in a pile; grass is even higher. You allow him to lounge about. You avoid your friends because you do not want them to see your house. Complaining about that pain he made-up, with the remote in the other hand. Ready to eat, ready to sleep he's the one you cannot beat. They are a Lazy Man.

Some have wondering eyes they will never be satisfied. They have more than they can count. Soon as one moves in one moves out. They do not care if you know, if you do not like it you can hit the door. They prefer you weak with no esteem. Be forewarned respect is something you will never receive. They are the Womanizer Man.

There is some looking for that queen. The golden throne they are willing to share. Give you the world if they could. They will look for virtuous in you. They will provide they will protect. Having a strong connection is essential. He will be handy to fix your needs. Sharing dreams sharing desires will make you his superstar. Understanding and kind who know all good things comes in time. No need to be perfect he will take you as you are. You will be the only one that catches his eyes. Some has been taken advantage of, now they are caution on whom to choose. If he choose you, blessed you will be. This is a Good Man.

Last night

I dream of you, a love that was true. It was only a fantasy. I formed your face I controlled your words. You knew what to say. You did everything in the right way. Last night I dream of you. You held me tight as I slept through the night. Oh, what a fantasy dream I had of you last night.

Beauty

The garment I wear or the length of my hair will not symbolize beauty. It will not be recognize by a smile or dress size. The side of the track will not determine the way I should look or the way my attitude should act.

What you will perceive is all the love my heart shows. This is the beauty I demonstrates,

I know the beauty I portray. Beauty upon a face changes every day. My beauty is a special find, an unconditional love that stands out.

Deadbeat

Here you come again with a different excuse on why you are late. Every time I have to call you out so you can pick a date. I probably would not hear a word if I did not have to track you down.

Whine; whine that is all you do. Complain; complain about the problems you are going through. Even have the nerves to try to blame me for your misfortune. Stop doing wrong maybe your life will change. Stop doing wrong maybe your life will turn around. Your child getting older and has notice the truth.

Get an attitude when the court has to make contact with you. Now, you are wondering on what to do. Surprise: surprise I am getting calls from you. Yeah, yeah it takes them to make you do what you suppose to do. Keep it steady, stay with the pace. Just do what the judge say.

Give *instruction* to a wise *man*, and he will be yet wiser: teach a just *man*, and he will increase in learning.

(Proverbs 10:9)

Caramel Princess

Beautiful caramel girl, her hopes and dreams are immeasurable. A little naive to the world and its entire means. I wish I could forever wrap my arms around you to keep you out of harm's way. Please listen well as I quote you words and I pray it will guide you to make you strong and insightful.

I am not perfect this you know. Nevertheless, my love for you continues to grow. You are my inspiration, my pride and my joy. Never fear your mother is here, when times seem rough lean on me. You are my child and I love you my dear.

Forgiveness

Sometimes we allow anger to overpower our mind. Powering our heart making it hard to forget and incapable to forgive. Giving it full authority of our thinking. A decision maker in our lives. So much, rage that we are not able to let nothing go. Forgiveness is for peace: a soul rescuer. There are steps to complete in order to clear it from the heart. Asking the Lord to forgive you and also them on what was done.

Have you ever wonder why it is so hard to forgive others. Have you really thought about what really cause the hurt in your heart? Remember what you said; remember your actions to make things so bad. We seem to over look our own faults. Putting the blame on everyone forgetting our part.

Before we forgive others, we must first forgive ourselves. We made a mistake with wrong judgments or wrong words. We pray that we learned from it and hope we never do that again. Forgive yourself before you forgive others, because guilt is a growth that goes deep within.

Approach it with an open mind; understand that not all will be kind. Remember you are cleansing your soul. You need to do this if you are seeking peace. Understanding that their heart is still healing and forgiveness is sometimes hard for others to do. Forgive them so you may have some stillness in your life.

This time when I pray

This Time when I pray I will ask for nothing. I will not ask for a blessing for a good deed I have done. This time when I get on my knees, I will not ask for a miracle because of my greed. This time when I pray I will make sure, the complete time is praising you.

I will not ask you to watch over my family and me. I will not pray for leaders to stop the wars and bring forth peace. This time when I pray, I will only be praising thee. As much as you do, how dare I ask for something new? When I pray this time I will not be trying to honor me by sharing what I am giving hoping to receive.

This time when I pray, I will concentrate on thanking you. I will clear my mind so my thoughts will only be for you. I do not need that fame and glory so this I will not ask. This time when I pray, I will not ask you to heal me. This time when I pray it will be sweet, it will not be about me. This time when I pray I will repeat thanking only you.

Release the snooze

It is time to wake up my people. Wake up and get going. Once again, a new day is upon you. What are you going to do? You were woken to learn and to teach. You were woken to give and to receive a blessing. A new starting point will begin when you stop nodding. It is time to wake up and get going.

Do not take the life you have on earth for granted. Do something meaningful with your gift, with your life. When you snooze, you shorten your time. When you snooze, you will truly lose and you still have nothing done. Useful time was waste because you chose to snooze. Wake yourself up and get something going.

Bang Bang (Harsh reality)

Sixteen and got your life screwed up. Red or blue which color has chosen you. Bang Bang is the sound you do not run from. Iron bars are too weak to alarm you. Mommy staying up late praying you are safe and out of the bullet way. Bang Bang can get you dead because another color has a gun to your head.

Feeling you are not loved your gang is now the new family. In your heart, you know they are the ones that will slice you. Bang Bang can get you departed because of the colors that you wear. It is time to get out and get your life right before it get too late. The next Bang Bang you hear could have you on your deathbed.

Can't get right

No matter how much you have tried.

No matter how much you have prayed.

Seem like you cannot get right.

No matter how much you have cried.

No matter how much you have pleaded.

Seem like you cannot get right.

No matter how smart you think, you are.

No matter how elite you appear to be.

If your heart is not pure, you will never be completely right.

If I did not pray

Where would I be if I did not get on my knees to pray to thee? I would have not made it without praying to you. Not having any faith to believe in. Not sure if you will pull me out when facing the pit. Be lost with despair and barely holding on. Confuse and wounded from being victimize from attacks. If I did not pray, I would not have you to praise.

Unable to decide on the right path to take when it comes to making spiritual choices. If I did not pray, habits will have their way. I will be weak to the unknown, accepting whatever comes my way. If I did not pray, it would mean I do not believe in you and all the wonderful things you do.

As Is

Who you see is who I am with no papers and no receipt. Straight from a master hand. Molded and formed to be as is. You might see some damage by the way I keep some feelings to myself. Only because I have met so many that was so finicky. No plastic no gel is needed to enhance the quality of how real I can be. No return is necessary I have no problem leaving if you cannot accept me for me.

Giving Away Time

Their time is now your time if you submit to it. When you allow yourself to step into their space, you are giving away precious time. Time you should not be wasting if it does not help others or benefit you. Do not give away your time if you are not strong enough to handle stressful situation. Stop submitting your energy to an insolent case.

You gave up some time that will never be back. A chance to do something different, something better is now gone. If it is not for you let it go. Do not allow it to drain you, to take away your time from creating something new. Avoid it, ignore it, and move on. Every minute, every hour of our life must be counted for.

The Lord blesses us with 24 hours. There is time to praise, time to rest. Time to nourish our body, time to help and to be productive. Whatever is left is up to you. Use it wisely, because they are not the one that will judge you. So, stop allowing them to control your time.

Help me to understand

Body filled with toxic clogging up your mind. Hatred and revenge is preventing common sense to creep in. Help me to understand why I should believe what you are dishing when there is not any logic coming out of your mouth.

With the smell of rum reeking from your tongue and the bible under your arm. You have the audacity to preach about what need to be done for us to be as one. Up and down is how your emotion is running from that natural high. Unable to see the truth because of the redness in your eye. Let me take this in help me to understand, how does this make you a man with a plan?

Through The Storm
(Feeling your thoughts and pain of Katrina)

So swift so quickly it came. Warning was given but still was not sure, still believed I have enough time. Praying repeatedly to remain secure. Through the storm I held on, I held on with all my breath and some had none left. Patiently I waited with the feared I might give in that I might have to give up.

Got so weary and so tired that all I could do was cry. Wondering around hoping I will be found. Hunger for a thirst and dreading the nights because of the lack of light. Innocent children confused this is something I wish they did not have to endure.

Through the storm, I needed peace and Lord you saved me. I lost the things I bought. You called home a few, but you rescued me so I may tell of this trial. Through the storm with such a gentle name, my place called home is not the same. Katrina, I never thought you would bring so much pain. It will be some time before I get back on my feet. This battle I will defeat this will not take the best of me.

Who Am I

Many have tried to personate me. Still lacking that style and grace. They believe they can take my place. My attitude is straight forward and to the point. Representing womanhood to the utmost is what I was taught. No need to bow your respect is all I demand. Standing beside my man is where you will find me. Letting him know I have his back. To the top steadily we will climb.

Who am I, I am the highest of all women? I am his queen. He is my protector, my warrior, bred to win. With Mandingo skin a godly heart within. Our kingdom is our home. Mind and spirit we are allied. Together we will rule this land. No distraction can remove me from my throne. I am, who I am, I am a Queen.

Caught Up

She was voted homecoming queen one of the beautiful girls they have ever seen. Warm hearted, sweet and kind. Going to college was on her mind all the time. As high school sweethearts, they seem to be the perfect team. He knew what to say to make her stick around. Hiding that jealous streak, he wanted her all for his self. Lost his drive to make it to the top, needed her company to make him feel sheltered. She did not run from that right hook. She thought this was love because she saw how her mother remained when daddy did the same.

Lost her identity caught up in the game. Had no idea this came with a price? She saw so many family and friends fallen by the waste side. So many times, she cried out hoping he will stop. She loved him more than she loved herself. Now she caught up as her beautiful appearance begins to disappear. Mind all congested from that drug she chose to try.

She tried to run and hide but when found he brought her back. She always knew she was trap. Felt so weak and alone even hope was gone. Constantly on her knees please Lord save me. Day by day, she prayed that he hears her words. Give me strength to leave; this is not the love for me. How she wishes she could hit him back, instead she knew the best way to win this fight was to just pack her bags and get out. With pain in her heart but a smile on her face, she finally realizes this was that day to walk away.

Destiny calling

Unable to make a plan your fate has been place in your hand. You are afraid to challenge your purpose or to use your gift. Your destiny has been calling. Avoiding and ignoring is very easy to do. You change the focus when the subject comes up.

Fear is not a spirit but you let it in. Terrified of success you doubt your greatness the person you are destiny to be. Surrender yourself to your purpose that you have concealed.

Think you know me

Southern girl with some flare. Every woman all wrap up in one.
Quiet and polite until you want to act as if your game is tight. Are
you judging me because of what you heard from an unreliable source
that got the big head? Baby please you do not know me. Sweet and
innocent is all part of my gentle side. Loveable and carefree comes
from the confident I have in me. Do not even try to cross me. I am
even smooth enough to let a couple of them slide. Then I would have
to let my Savior cut you down to size. It is cool if you feel you have
to talk behind my back. Do not twist the logic when I snap you back.
Did I forget to mention there is a little hood that you misunderstood?

Just because I visit, your spot does not mean it's you I am checking
out and it definitely does not mean I think you are hot. I am here just
to whisper a little knowledge in your ear; it has nothing to do with
your appear. Oh, you still think you know me. I can be a flirt and a
tease; it does not mean I want you. I assort my associates with care. I
will not deal with hooey and negative spirits. An opportunism who
see me as an easy ride thinking you seen my vulnerable side.
I admit I can be a little green, that just the silliness in me.
Nevertheless, have no doubt I am a dealing whiz and I can handle
whatever is out. Have no time for your drama, because you feel your
life has stumble. Still think you know me, baby please. What I shared
is just the tip of that iceberg. To learn me is to know me. To know me
is to allow me to do me.

Believe

He has shown you what he can do. Yet you still find it hard to believe. When that bit of doubt slips in your faith becomes thin. Believe that miracles still exist.

All he asks is to have faith and to believe. Time after time day after day, he is with you showing you his wonders and still waiting on you to believe what you feel, what you see.

All is possible when you believe.

Each new day

I thank the Lord for this new day, a day that was not guarantee. Should I continue with my same routine or should I change and try something different to better me.

Each new day is another chance; each new day is brand new. Never knowing what it will bring. It is time to get it right before I rest for the night.

Each new day is another chance for me to prepare my soul in order to enter those pearly gates. This new day was given to me to forgive all those past hurt. A chance to get my life right and to put my belongings in order.

Each day is another chance to say I love you to the ones who thought I never did. It will be another day to say Mother, Father I thank you for all that you have done.

Each new day is another chance.

Each new day is another chance.

Use it wisely, because each new day only comes once.

I thank you

For all that you do to show the wonderful grace of you. Watching the sunset is a miracle to behold or seeing a blossom bloom. Took for granted the littlest things you do. How can we forget to thank you for the smallest blessings that you bring?

I thank you for alerting me before danger. I thank you for the smallest things. When, I find my keys after being lost. I thank you for showing me what is needed is already in my house and I do not have to go out. I thank you for waking when my alarm will not. I thank you for granting me with these small blessings as well as the large.

Divided

One by one.

Side by side.

When one fall, we will all fall down.

Together we stand together we must embrace all.

One by one.

An inch apart

Once holding hands

Now fisted they ball.

Together we stand, divided we fall, one by one.

Until there is none

Forgotten Mission

Check you out standing so proud in that spot light. Who do you think are? You forgot what the mission was regarding too. You forgot why you were picked, and why you were chosen. Were you one of the greedy who jumped in front of the line? Saw all the prizes that were pouring down that you faked your way to the top.

Do not look surprise; you know what I am preaching about. It is not about the mighty anymore, now it is about all the gold your pockets can hold. What happen to the way it use to be when true leaders were call?

You are not the only ones pledge to the promise land. You feel so great because you on national TV. Because, of your behavior so many have swayed. So many you befriended is now convince you will oversee their way. Do not forget the mission, change back to the way it use to be.

Heart vs. Mind

For a while, I have been allowing my heart and mind to go to war. Battling over what is right, combating on which is the strongest. My heart was not prepared and it was hidden on the shelf. The mind played games thought it was slick with all the little tricks. It learned to master words so it was one-step ahead of the rest.

Keeping the heart out of view saving it was the best option to do. Never thought it would be you. Every now and then, it would show. Nevertheless, the mind would rush in with it oh no's. It will remind the heart to be careful, to watch out. Do you really want to be torn into two? Once again, the mind won. The mind was having fun, poor little gentle heart did not know what to do. It was feeling lonely it wanted to get off the shelf it needed affection too.

The heart was wondering if it could just sit upon the sleeves would it be a safe space to be. It just wanted to breathe too. It wanted to look around and see what is out there for me. The heart tried a different strategy. I would not let the mind lead, they must work together. Day after day, working as one allowing the mind to feel them out. If the spirit is right deep within the heart will let out a shout. It took some time it took some years the mind and heart finally found someone that is genuine.

Brought me up to this day

I have been preparing for whatever comes my way. Not all has been great I must say. Growing stronger each and every day. Praying has strengthened me to handle life difficulties. I cannot let doubt run through my mind; it will take up too much of my time.

I will not worry about what you have to say or what you try to do. I have been preparing for this day. My faith has been building for this day. My purpose in life was planned and my gift is not limited to just this one.

Invincible is what I am trying to become. Higher and higher I must reach. I will not be troubled on what the doctor has to say. I will not fret if you do not like me. I will not be bother if things do not go my way. I will not be concern if you do not understand. I will not let anything irritant me. I have been preparing for this day to use my faith in every way.

Behold, I am the Lord, the God of all flesh: is there any thing too hard for me?
(Jeremiah 32:27)

Circling Blessings

I do not know why you are here. I do not know why you came. I pray you are able to stay awhile until your new journey has to begin. It is true we do not always know why people come into our lives. If we example our situation carefully what is currently going on. We will understand the reasons when they leave.

I once heard we should look at what we have, not at what we had. Blessing comes in many forms. It can be your words, which you take time to share. It can be a simple joke, when a person is feeling down. Expressing a smile to a stranger is a blessing of its' own.
Just when you think no one is listening, when no one is watching, when you think no one cares, someone is there. Your life is prearranged and the Lord will arrange the right person to step in. Sometimes the one who just arrived in your life is there for a reason, even if it is for a quick minute.

Even if it is good or bad, a lesson will be learned. It might not be for you, your presence might have been for them. When you take time to bless one, the power of blessing is circling back to you. The more you pray, the more you love and the more you rotate blessings it will continue to grow.

Hold on

Feeling depress mind lost in space. Keep your head up and do not lose faith.

You can make it, and you can hold on. Remove that flown and show a smile.

Hold on and never give up, remember you are a well-built design. The Lord wants you to know you are not forsaken and he has not abandoned you. You are next in line.

He is mighty this we know. He blessed you with strength to make it easier to hold on. There are others weaker then you. He has many others that need him too.

Hold on and do not give up. He has his angels watching over you. Soon, he will answer your prayers too only if He feels it is right for you.

Hold on and do not let go. Use the faith you built up from the other trials you conquer, while you wait on the Lord to pull you through.

It's Time

At one time, my love was true for no one but you. Thinking you felt the same. Blinded by confusion by the things you do. I have taken off the shades so now I can see. I have focus more on your action to understand you better. Now I know your heart was not even there. Felt excited when I heard your voice and feeling exotic when I felt your touch. Thought this must be heaven on earth to have a love this great. Fill with bliss from the tenderness of your kiss.

I am strong enough to say what a fool I have been to let it go on so long. Two people together but I am the one who always felt alone. Thinking I am this Man queen, this is what I truly would say. Giving my all to make it work, thought you were here to stay. While my head was turned looking above, to thank my lucky stars. You were still looking for that Cinderella to fit that shoe. Not knowing you were looking at princess, someone who still has not arrived to my Queen status. They were missing the royal data.

It is a shame you never knew the one you were searching for was already staring you right in your face. Before, the clock - click another second. It is time to go it is time to move on. Too much time I have wasted. This fantasy is over I can admit.

I have no regrets for the love I gave, for the love I lost. It is time for me say goodbye. Because now I see, it was not me. You were too afraid to give your all. This love you do not deserve-it is time for you to hit the door. Playing these mind games made things change. One day you will see, all that time it was me.

Keep Going

When you are down and out keep going. When life throws a bow, keep going. When you reach a certain age you should expect changes and be prepared to handle them. Embrace them even if they are not to your approval. Everything in life is temporary so treat them that way the good and the bad.

When you're confronted with hatred know that it's only their fear of the love you have inside. Everyone cannot appreciate your love, everyone don't deserve your love. After trying after giving and you notice nothing in return, keep going.

Enjoy your life; find peace within your joy and your pain. It's only temporary it will pass. Don't let anything uncontrollable panic you. Keep going and walk with pride with your head to the sky. Keep going with a smile on your face.

Know when to let go and move on. When you are in unhealthy situation, let it go and keep going. Allow hurt to be your strength. The lord will give you your blessings but you have to recognize it to accept it. He will try to give it to you many times. If you are blind to what is true what is good maybe you don't deserve it. You should keep going.

Until you do right

Being low down and insensitive to others is not the way to be. Your life will never go right until you do right. Getting mad and upset is not the way to act. You cannot see, you do not notice how hate affects your life. Until you treat others with kindness, nothing will go right for you. Your pride is keeping you from saying sorry from all your wrongdoing and it is keeping you from something better. You cannot hurt others and still expect a blessing.

Wandering Spirits

Growing up we was told not to open the door to anyone and it stands true today. Who or what you invite into our home can influence our lives. There are wandering spirits around us the good and the evil. Angels are ministering spirits whom God has sent to help us and demons are menacing spirits whom Satan has sent to impede us. When you are at peace with yourself, your family, your house, you have a ministering spirit in your presence.

Just when you are comfortable and everything is going good, something unexpected happens. Because we understand, everyone is subject to trials. However, all of sudden the boat is rocked either by you, a stranger or someone you love. That is because someone has invited a menacing spirit into your life. Once that spirit comes into your home it will soon try to take control of your heart and mind by creating hateful thoughts and hateful action.

A ministering spirit represents peace and knowledge. They are here to protect and comfort you. A menacing spirit stirs up problems. They only need one person to pass it on. A person carries spirits, so welcome the right spirit into your life. Think before your act, your actions represent your spirit. Pray that the Lord always sent ministering angels into your life.

Lost Sistah

My sistah why have you lost your way? Looking for some direction, you are bouncing from here and there. A stressful and deadly lifestyle is where you will find yourself if you do not watch out. Not even trusting yourself when it comes to making decisions. Confident is what you lack. Lost your esteem, now you chose not to betray yourself as the queen who you was groomed to be.

You forgot that you are a mother, a sister, and a leader. You follow whoever welcomes you to join in. Find yourself my beautiful lost sistah. At what age do you realize it is time for a change? It is time to use the map the Lord has supplied you with. It is time to learn your purpose on this earth.

On your last days can you say you have lived your dream, at least tried? Hiding the true, you hoping no one will see. Are you teaching your daughter the real meaning of being a queen? Teaching your son the way a queen should be treated. Your action is the examples they will remember.

We are the same. Different color may show on our face what we share in our heart is what must blend. Hating on each other is not the way it should be. When one is down, reach out your hand to lift them up. When their mind is wondering lends an ear and let them know you are there. So many have lost themselves in the struggle not caring you let yourself go. Take some time to rediscover and get back your life.

Say His Name

Shout it Say it do what you must.
Give his name praise.
Spell it Write it let the world know.
He is whom you claim.
Never be ashamed in saying his name.
Every blessing you received you
should give his name the praise.
Glorify it and appreciate his name.
His name represent deity oh mighty.

Thinking back

On this brisk cool day thinking about a love that got away. Missing it without any notice how slowly it happens. All the lovely memories always start with a smile. The more I sat the more it was recalled. Thinking back to all the heartache that was involved. Never imagined it would be the main condition when it came to loving you.

Thinking back to all the harsh words that were said from the mouth I use to love to kiss. Thinking back to all the secrets that were told. Our friendship was split in two by the deception of you. Thinking back makes me wonder what I seen in you.

Thinking back to all the times I cried from waiting on you to come around. Believed this so call relationship was on solid ground. Thinking back helped me to get over you.

Soulful Soul

My Soul is so fervor yet my attitude remain cool. Once you connect with my spirit be ready because it will hold on to everything. A soulful soul I have snapping my fingers rocking my head to that jazz. Dress so clean smelling so fresh looking exceptional. Your first expression of what you see will make you wish you were me.

My soul is so soulful, so soulfulness is my soul. I will give no smack and I will not take any back. Sexy, classy and sassy is how I am identified. Flirtiest to the bone is how I handle my home when I am alone with that man I call my own.

My soulful soul is deep inside of me so spiritual and carefree. My love is strong with a mighty hold. A love you cannot let go. I am not trying to brag. I am not trying to boast. I am one in a million don't you know. I am a super woman not a woman that wonders. I do not stress about today and I am not going to worry about tomorrow. Placing my faith with thee keeps my mind at ease. Before I end before I close remember every woman possesses that soulful soul.

Your Blessings

We so often pray for things and when it is received it is ours. No man can take it away. We pray for a new car. That car will be the newest and sharpest on the street. We keep it clean and drive in pride. We pray for the biggest house on the market and invite everyone to visit.

When we feel we cannot find the right person to love. We get on our knees and pray for that mate. Someone no one can take away. We claim for these things to never leave that it is here to stay.

We understand there will be good and bad times in our lives. There will be trials we must go through. Time has now pass that car is so expensive we spending our income on the payments and repairs until we lose it. That lovely house is taking away family time because of all the overtime at work. That soul mate is having affairs in your present with abusive disrespect.

Yet you do not understand, once again you are on your knees asking why. The Lord will bless you with these things to teach you. The Lord will allow you to claim these things to teach you because he does answer prayers. Sometimes your blessing is not his blessings for you. It is just a lesson to be learned. What you want is not always what the Lord wants you to have. When you are, bless with certain things. It will not stress you out. It will not cause you to suffer. The Lord's blessings are perfect and bountiful.

Look closely at the things you have claimed or prayed for in your life. Is it truly for you? May the Lord continue to bless you with wisdom, knowledge and open sight so you may recognize the difference?

My momma prays for me

Before I was born still a bundle in her womb, she was praying for me. Praying that I will be healthy and safe as I grew. That all my desires and dreams come true.

Even as a teen when my peers tried to pressure me to try something that will cause me harm she was silently praying that my life would not fumble. Hoping her teaching made a breakthrough. She knew I still had goals I needed to pursue.

Heartache, joy, or pain her prayers remain. Watching me as I changed my momma prays for me. With her faith and mines, I am refining.

Perfect fit

From the ribs of Man, Woman was created to accommodate him. Not always seeing eye to eye which was sometimes understandable. They just knew they were a pair as one. They shared a soul a spirit. As I study the meaning of this, I come to realize the true meaning of a soul mate. I understand why a man states that they are looking for their rib the perfect fit.

A soul mate is the connection of one bringing back to make a whole. A perfect fit is not saying we are perfect in whom we are. As you unite being perfect to work together. Finding a mate of the soul is not easy it can take years. When you find that mate, your soul will now. You will feel a connection; you will know what each other is thinking. Even feel what they are doing without being there.

Understand you cannot be alone on this, you might feel you found that soul mate. The other must feel for you too. A perfect fit will have the gift of communication, the joy of laughter. Someone strong enough to handle the highs and the lows. The perfect fit will bring forth peace. The importance of a soul mate is the word soul, a spiritual binding of the soul for the man and woman. Never forget the Lord hands are on this pairing.

Only he can separate the perfect fit. Only he knows who is right for you and only he will join you back to your perfect fit.

Not my business

I hope understand if you need me I will be there. In a case of an emergence, you can count on me. If you need an ear I have one to share. Just do not get me caught up with your unnecessary qualms that you are dealing with. When you know you too should not be there. Your lacking of confidence keeps you from leaving it alone.

I have my own business I do not need anyone else. Yes, I heard the rumors spreading about and I hope you get it straighten out. Staying at peace is what I require. I have no time to get in between hearsay chat. Being serenity is best for me, so keep that drama to yourself.

Journey Ended

I strutted by so proudly with my seductive smile. I had no plan on sticking around. Falling for you was very easy to do. Crossing paths was destiny from the stars. Eventually I knew you would have my heart. Time passes when you are learning someone new. Sharing secrets and desires is what I admired about you.

Even though we felt this was too good to be true. Our hearts had their own personal gatekeeper. Feelings was in safekeeping so deep inside. Fearing a repeat from the past that our heart will be split apart. Therefore, we went through the motion taking each day with caution. We were still causing pain when there should not be. Causing heartaches just for the sake of it. Commitment was easy to say but hard to do. Dreaming of the future was so much fun. Picturing us growing old made us laugh as we made our plans. It is a shame it had to end because a new journey had to begin.

Had to make a detour this route is not safe anymore. Confusion was mapped and I saw the warning signs up ahead. Bumpy road can be dangerous for the heart. Now I am driving with care this type of love is not real. Cover with protection from head to toe yet the pain stills show. You got too comfortable thinking anything goes. The fire went out when you blew out the flame. This journey had to end maybe one day we can be friends again.

Against All Odds

You have reached out your arms to the weak and weary. You shared your brawn shoulders to those who knew you would be there in time of need, asking for nothing in return. You live with the understanding that not all will value your worth. Some tried to take your kindness for granted. No matter what comes your way, you rely on the Holy Spirit for your guiding light.

Against any odds, you have stood strong. Some may try to slow down your goals by trying to make you lose focus. They do not realize who you are. You are a noble king, a descendant of a higher being.

Against the odds, you did not allow chains to hold you down. You do not allow criticism to lower you. Your character is of great knowledge and wisdom. That makes you differentiate from the rest. You are a prominent ebony man. Keep praying, being still and watch as your blessings pours in.

And whatsoever ye shall ask in my name, that will I do, that the Father may be glorified in the Son. If ye shall ask any thing in my name, I will do it.
(John 14:13-14)

You Are Ready My Brother

You are ready my brother have you not notice the electrifying energy surrounding your presence. Pay no mind to the negative energy; it is just trying to block you from your destiny of greatness. You have been chosen so get prepared for battle. The little things you have done are nothing compared to what is ahead. Fear not my brother you are ready.

You have fortified your mind with prayer because the wicked will try to discourage you. Your body is now solidifying to carry the weight of a mountain. Fear not my brother our heavenly father knows how much you can bear. Your spirituality has strengthened because of your steadfast of your beliefs. The only weapon you need is the word of God.

You are ready my brother fear not of those things that lure in the shadow of darkness. Fear not of the things that try to bait you. Fear not of the enticements of evil things. You see my bother you are ready. Face the mirror my brother you will see your armor, you will see your shield, and oh yes my brother you will see your crown. My brother in spirit you are ready. May the power of our glorious God guild you through the unknown and protect you from harm.

Sunshine

Hot like fire.

Brighter than the stars.

You are like the sun that shines.

Warming my heart as you make me beam.

I am your sunshine and you are mines.

Staying Focus

We understand staying focus on the important issues of life
is not always easy to do. Distractions can come along and
direct you off your path. With a quick swift, have you drifting
up stream. Remember you still have things undone.
undone. Stay focus and keep your eyes on the prize.
The package might look small. The content has a much
bigger surprise. You might embark on something new trying
to hang with the crew. Even if your peers say, try it.
You are intelligent enough to know that is not for you. You
have something better to do.
Stay focus; Stay clear of those illusions that quickly
disappear. Your endurance keeps you strong. Stay on target
and to the point. Stay headstrong to your beliefs that you
are bless for greatness. Rest when needed, and then precede for
the seeds you have planted will be bountiful oh yes indeed.

It will happen

Life is not perfect. Circumstances will bring us down. Problems seem to always be around. I am sure you have learned everything is not good sometime dilemmas can make you strong, but you must be willing to grasp on.

As we grow, we realize we will go through a cycle. Faith is necessary to handle life tribulations. As we grow, we realize there will be unavoidable situation that will cause us to cry. As we grow, we realize the choices we made cannot be reverse.

You cannot be scare to try something different because you are unsure you are unable to finish. So stop worry and stop stressing acting like this is new. It will happen repeatedly before your life is through.

You will be prepared before you go through it. It is already in the plan. You are his child and slowly you will do steps to help you develop your strength of your spirit. If you acknowledge that problems will occur and allow your faith to pull you through the wiser you will be when it happens again.

I had that dream too (yes, we did)

In you his spirit live through making the dream a reality. With the same confident voice, you speak and I listen. You motivate me; you inspire me to do much more. Now I can explore several avenues because you have opened more doors.

When I see your faces standing in once a forbidden place, I can say I too had that dream. A dream of being free. Free from hate because of the darkness on my skin. Free to vision a reality of something they said should not be. A chance of modification has come. A chance to join as one, you see I am not afraid of this transformation. The old ways need to remain in those old days.

I had that dream too that Martin spoke of when freedom will ring. From the streets below, to the house on the hill every man and every woman can live in harmony. I had that dream too of healing this so call land of opportunity, which all people may live evenly. This is what hope you speak of means to me.

You have brightened the eyes of a child who stop believing in goals that high. Yes, we can hope for a better nation for all races. Yes, we can hope of being release from restraints. No more of holding us back as we try to hold it down. This is what hope means to me when I had that dream last night.

You are stronger enough to look over the negativity they tried to say. From the past years, we learned familiarity does not guarantee greatest from a chief. What our heart desire is something fresh, something new. This is what we distinguish with you.

Many do not understand the vows that were made. Having hope is only the first phase. After years of suffering under a system that has kept us, down. It will take some time to rebound. Watching and waiting anticipating a mistake. I hope that one day they too have confidence in you. They will see you were chosen to be.

They assumed we were not ready for you. White, black, yellow and brown have proven they are wrong. We all have endured some sort of pain for this gain. Yet the struggle lingers on. I had that dream too of marching to victory, a dream of unity. You have been claim because you were prayed on.

You have uplifted us that we now have a chance to live better from the visions you shared from your heart and mind. You have opened our eyes to brighter skies. Once again, they underestimated your strength. I am even surer you are the best selection to lead us to what was promise. To have a prospect of being prosperous and free.

Black, white, yellow and brown we all have been waiting on someone like you. You see we all have dreamed that dream so our children may grow up in serenity. This is what hope means to me. This year is the start of that day when everyone that has dream that dream becomes reality.

Way of Thinking

You have planted that seed of doubt and now that is all your mind thinks. Feel bad luck is controlling your life. Feeling your blessings has passed you by. Even your health and living behavior is negative. You cannot count all the occasions you have been saved through your faith. Yet you live disappointed because opportunities is not going your way.

Change your way of thinking to positive thoughts. Not everything will go the way you expected which is all part of life. There will be good times and the letdowns, do not get discourage.

Your mind and your tongue have great influence over your life and under your control. You have to think, speak and live positive. Do not allow your tongue to speak of illness and misfortune because your negative mind of thinking may cause you to claim it. You know you are blessed. Well think and act that way. Let no one tell you it is not possible believe it.

Sibling rivals

Brothers and sisters the same source they came. Loving and caring that how they grew. Older and wiser they proclaim, if they parents could see them they would be ashamed. Maybe this time water is thicker than the blood that is shared.

Distant they became when they start calling each other names. No compassions have hardened the heart. Always competing by bragging on what you got. Feeling you is blessed while others have lack. One by one now, the number is few. Come together to the love you knew. Strangers you become siblings are the past you knew.

Healing prayer

Lord hear my prayer.
Something is going on that I am in
need of you. I am crying out for a healing
from all this suffering and pain.
Heal me Lord from top to bottom,
from my inside and out. From this trial let
me be that testimony. Your name
is above them all and with faith I will not fall.
No, matter what they do or what they said,
your touch is the cure, my therapist that heals.
I have no need to worry and stress because
I know I am blessed. I will quietly wait until
you finish what you have to do to make me new.
It is you I lean on and who I must come to. With you there
will be no mistakes. Fix me Lord on this day.
Amen

Don't Give Up

When times get rough and it seem like it is so hard to bear do not give up. I know you feel you have tried your best and it still not good enough. Do not give up and do not let depression permeate.

Raising your hands up high and questing why. Feeling forsaken, please do not give up now.

This is not the time to give up hope to have doubt in your life. Hold on and stay strong with courage. Whatever your trials may be do not stray away.

Do not feel sad and start wondering why you do not have what other have or the abilities to do what others can. Not every blessing is the same. Not everybody gets blessings at the same time. Nevertheless, you are bless just hold on and do not give up.

Girlfriend

I feel your pain the struggles you endure. Raising your children all alone was not part of the diagram. Thought you had a real man to help you out. Do not look down and do not give up you are stronger then you think you are.

You know the power of prayer and now your children have notice what prayer can achieve. Everything will be just fine. A blessing comes with time. You are doing your best and right now that is all you can do. Do not look down and do not give up are you stronger then you think you are.

Learn to depend on faith, not family and friends. I am sure you are tired and there will be times you have to cry, let it out and bounce back. Do not look down and do not give up are you stronger then you think you are.

Blackness

The unseen

Darker then shadow never compared to white. The luck that is bad. The dirtiest sheep of the pack.

Shady, hopeless, wicked and a sneak. A nightfall that has not been guided by the light.

Bottomless pit with no way out. Just an unfortunate to be dark-skinned, a curse to mankind.

Once a slave to masters. Now a slave to the system, because of the color of the skin. I will not be characterize by my blackness.

In a blink of an eye (For Jackie)

I often remembrance on all the special times we spent laughing, joking and enjoying every moment that we shared. Took life for granted thinking it will always last. Not only were we family we also were best of friends. In a blink of an eye the moments change, you were not acting the same.

I wish I had that miracle cure to help you heal. I wish I knew something to have kept you here. I still feel your presence even though it been some years. I thank the Lord for allowing my beautiful angel of flight to continue to watch over me. I know we did not always see eye to eye, but within a blink of an eye you left me here.

For days I was sad. For day I cried, for day I felt so empty inside. I hope you know I miss you so. One day soon, we will be together again. I have to remove any hate from my heart. Follow his words and walk in his path. If I do what I suppose to do, I will be able to see you.

In a blink of an eye, life can change. We have to cherish each moment as if it was our last before it pass. I am not being sad not anymore, because I know you are at peace. I smile each time I think of you and the all the silly things we use to do. I am pleased with myself knowing we had no hard feeling before you left. I am pleased that we still acted like family to the very end.

In a blink of an eye you suddenly died. My grieving days are gone. I am sure you want me to live my life on. You will never be forgotten your spirit lives on so deep inside my heart.

Find Me

Why do you search are you like me? Are you tired of the shucking and jiving? Tired of the same oh games. Would it ever change? Are you like me hoping that one day it would be through? No more searching to do. Find me if that is true. I have been here waiting on you. Faith in your spiritual belief is what you must have in order to make this last.

If you search for unconditional, well so do I. If you search for something that is long lasting, well me too. If you search for a friend to help, you cope. This is what you will find if you look for me.

Tranquility

I feel so peaceful when I bow my head in prayer. Like a child I cried out. Without saying a word, I allow you to hear my heart. With my eyes closed, I can feel your arms surrounding me and instantly a soft whispering sound comes from your voice telling me it will be all right. The most peaceful time in my life is when I pray to thee.

Just the beginning

Have no need to complain on how long it took. You knew the right time to come with this blessing. I was not surprise, I was not shock, but I was amazed feeling so bless.

I prayed on it and left it alone. I will not question it and I will not doubt it with what ifs' thoughts. Once again you have blessed me with what I needed.

I have this feeling stirring in my soul that this is just the beginning. With you, that there will be so much more.

Oh Heavenly Father

Oh Heavenly Father, hear my prayer! I come to thee on bended knees. Once again, another trial I must face. Always different from the rest. I know what I must do; I have to look toward you. I know I have no need to worry no need to stress. However Lord I am drain from these tests. I understand it brings me closer to you. I look at my life and all the things I have been through.

Thought my trials were punishments since they were more than just a few. As I grew, I finally knew the truth. My heart is good my spirit is strong and now I know why my trials went on and on. Not because of wrong but to built my faith with you.

Oh Heavenly Father, hear my prayer! From nothing you pulled me through. You remind me of the past of what I have struggled through that this should be nothing new. I made it before with you. Thanking only you oh Heavenly Father for strengthening me. When my heart aches when my mind wonder and my eyes flood.

Thanking only you oh Heavenly Father for holding me. When others turn their back and when others put my name to shame. Teach me oh Heavenly Father that my trials are blessings. In order to move closer to you to reach a higher level of spirituality I must pass these tests.

Fear not, O land; be glad and rejoice: for the Lord will do great things.
(Joel 2:21)

No doubts

My faith has power there is no doubt. Going through many ups and down from living my daily life. I have found my strength from trusting in his word. It took the trials to show me I should not have any doubts, just to wait and let him work it out.

No doubts will creep upon my thoughts when I know you have all authority over this earth. Your name is above all names. There is no need to have doubt. I will show acceptance, and be submission to your will. No doubts should cross my mind I trust you without any doubts.